Answering That of God in our Children

Harriet Heath

—— Pendle Hill Pamphlet 315 ——

About the Author

Harriet Heath is the mother of three and grandmother of five. Having grown up in a Methodist parsonage, she became a Quaker only after graduating from college. Implementing Quaker values while living and working with children became part of her spiritual journey. Now trained as a psychologist, she works with parents and families through the counseling service of the Family Relations Committee and the Religious Education Committee, both of the Philadelphia Yearly Meeting. She frequently contributes to the Parents Corner in the *Friends Journal*. She has also taught and worked as a school psychologist in public and Friends schools. She is a member of Radnor Meeting.

The recognition of the need for this pamphlet and its writing has evolved over several years. The ideas have grown out of working with children and through discussions with parents and colleagues. Special thanks go to all those who have kindly taken time to read and comment on the manuscript, especially to the author's two daughters, Wendilee and Annemarie.

The author has two hopes for this essay: one, that it will give parents and other care-givers insights as to how Quaker values can guide their daily lives with children and two, that it will continue our search as a community for greater understanding as to how to answer that of God in everyone, even in our children.

About the Artist

The oil painting on this pamphlet's cover and the line drawings of children in the text are by artist Wendilee Heath O'Brien. She is mother of Ben and Luke and lives at Pendle Hill.

Request for permission to quote or to translate should be addressed to Pendle Hill Publications, Wallingford, Pennsylvania 19086-6099.

ISNB 0-87574-315-3

Library of Congress catalog card number 94-067381

June 1994: 2,500

I asked when my children were young, "In what ways are our Quaker beliefs relevant to our lives with children?" I hear the same question being asked today.

This pamphlet is my response to that query. It grows out of my Quaker beliefs, my experiences rearing my children and watching my grandchildren grow, and out of my training in child development.

The Quaker belief in the Inner Light has given me values by which I wish to live and guide my children. It has not given me the "nitty gritty" information I need to be a parent. For this information I have turned to psychology and child development. Michael Rutter wrote in *A Measure of Our Values*:

> Religion is important in its definition of values and, in that, it provides no clash with science. Quite the opposite. Science *cannot* define social purposes and values. . . . Religious values determine goals but they cannot provide for decisions on the best means of reaching them.[1]

By discussing and illustrating how religion and psychology have come together in a unifying, meaningful and useful way for me, I hope this pamphlet will prove helpful to others who live and work with children and encourage them to share as they find their answers to the opening query.

"Walk cheerfully over the world," Fox wrote, "answering that of God in every one."[2]

I've always liked the advice. It is merry, warm and friendly.

It speaks of what has become a basic belief of Quakerism. There is that of God in every person.

Trying to apply the advice brought only confusion.

"To what do I answer, that is in every person?" I've wondered through the years. How was I to recognize "that of God" or "The Inner Light" which is the phrase I tend to use?

The question "to what do I respond?" needled me not only because it related to how I lived with others but because of its relevance to my living with and guiding children. If there is that of God, an Inner Light, in every person, does that include children? If so, at what age does that Light appear? And how does my belief in Its Presence in my children affect my task of guiding them?

I've asked this of parents. Where do you see that of God, the Inner Light, in your children? After some thinking one answered, "I see it when they are asleep." "Yes, of course they look so peaceful and angelic when asleep," I thought. Another described her child when intent on a project, eyes sparkling, slight frown, as she worked to get the building of blocks balanced just right. Another described his child dancing, keeping the beat, bending and twisting, with sparkling eyes and shining face. The essence of their being seems there shining through. They seem in tune with the universe. And I thought to myself, but can we see the Inner Light when they are whining under foot, refusing to do their homework, and/or having a temper tantrum in the middle of the supermarket? Is It there then, too?

Is that of God evident, for instance, in my grandchildren as I hear them fighting over a favorite toy? Do I, as the adult watching over them, have a role? Should I take some action regarding their fighting? I know that hitting will soon begin. And can I manage to walk cheerfully when having to deal with the homework, the temper tantrum and the fighting?

Our answers to these kinds of questions influence how we guide our children, how we discipline them. Our answers come from our beliefs about children, about human nature and about the divine.

The Puritans are a good example of how parental beliefs influence parental behavior. They believed that children were born evil, born in sin. The parents' responsibility was to make the children good so that they might gain salvation. The parents were to beat the evil out of their children; thus, the interpretation of the Biblical advice "Spare the rod and spoil the child" was to physically punish the child.

If we Quakers believe the Inner Light exists in every person and presumably, therefore, in every child, does it follow that the child is inherently good and can do no wrong? If the child is good and can do no wrong then the conclusion must be that the child needs no guidance. Our role is to be their friend, companion. Our experience with children makes most of us uncomfortable with this interpretation. And so we ask the question: Is the "Inner Light" in our children as well as in every person? And what are the implications of such a belief for how we live and work with children?

Recognizing that of God

Harold Loukes in his book, *Friends and Their Children* wrote: "We (Friends) start from an affirmation of the value of the child's humanity; not a naive belief that he is born good, but a belief that he can grow into goodness."[3]

"Goodness" speaks of values. It implies outward practice based on an inner belief about what is right. "Growing into" speaks of searching for truth, listening to the inner voice, using experience to confirm understanding, believing in continuing revelation. The process of seeking and testing truth and the capacity to choose and do good actions lie at the heart of Quakers' beliefs, a religion, therefore, of queries, not creeds. Harold Loukes wrote:

> We should in our religion as in other enquiries be honest to what we know, and put to the test of practice what we have been told, ready to reject it if it be false; and if it is true, follow it to the end. This is the "experimental" religion of early Friends: it is the belief in light.[4]

Quakers are wonderers. The wonderings take different forms. We wonder when we marvel at the beauty of the earth, the kindness of a friend, or the peace that comes with understanding another. We wonder when we search to understand why some are poor and others wealthy or the stream has become polluted on its way to the sea. We wonder when we seek to find what we should be doing in life or the best way to resolve a conflict.

Wonderings are an integral part of Quakerism. Quakerism assumes revelation is continuous, that all is not known or understood. Searching leads to understanding, to finding meaning. Quakerism is pervasive in that its leadings are to be followed daily. Seeking brings clearness as to the path to follow. Quakerism brings peace and joy. Marveling keeps us aware of the beauty and complexity of all that is around us and keeps us seeking. The wonderings provide a means for us to "grow into goodness." They are, I have come to see, an outward expression of the Inner Light, of that of God, of which George Fox spoke.

Music expresses it so well. The key is minor; the melody ends in a seventh—an incomplete musical statement. The words are adapted.

> I wonder as I wander out under the sky;
> The beauty and grandeur that around me doth lie;
> Will my soul find its calling in the vastness beyond?
> I wonder as I wander out under the sky.

Answering to That of God in Every Person

And to my surprise, believing that people can grow into goodness led me to be able to articulate what is the Inner Light, that of God, to which I can and do answer. I feel the closest to a person when we share the beauty of nature or a kindly deed, or when we seek to understand the dynamics of a situation, or we search to find an answer to a problem, or we attempt to comprehend how another sees an issue, or when that other shares with me how he or she came to believe as he or she does or arrived at the understanding he or she has obtained. The purpose of that searching is to find the best solution, what is right. Is it not also to grow into goodness? And when insight comes, there is such a feeling of "AH." "This is good." "This is right."

To that sharing, that searching and hopefully finding I respond, feeling in tune with the other. I experience a sense of wonder that it is so.

Quakerism drew me because it provided a community in which people can voice their concerns and questions. I cherish the freedom to search that Quakerism provides and its deep belief in continuing revelation. I am grateful for the community of members who share their wonderings and reflect back on mine. The importance of that community is not to be lost. Both

Quaker meeting and Friendly contacts provide a means for sharing one's own and others' wondering.

How often in meeting someone will rise to wonder, to marvel, at what is. Maybe it will be the call of the glory of trees standing straight and tall encouraging us, too, to stand straight and tall in facing life. Or maybe it will be people of the meeting reaching out to one going through a difficult period. Or maybe it will be in watching adolescents include younger children in their game of football, or in watching a sibling share a favorite toy. The capacity to marvel is one form of the wonder.

And one form of wonder is the Quaker search together to understand. Why do a people not have enough food now that were able to support themselves a couple of generations ago? We do not assume, "God wills it." We attempt to find the causes of discrimination, not call the discriminator "bad."

And part of wondering is seeking as when we ask "What can I do?" "What should my role be?" "Should I be caring for my newborn or working for social fairness?" "Should I work in the ghettos of my own country or in those in a developing nation?" "How can I live more in tune with my environment?" People seeking the path that is right for them seems also a sign of the Inner Light and is frequently expressed during our meetings for worship and for sharing.

To these forms of wonder, to me an outward expression of the Inner Light, of that of God of which George Fox wrote, I can answer. To my daughter as she marvels at the hues of the rocks and sea around her. I do not see the colors as she does; her sensitivity makes me more aware of them. I try to be in tune to the wonder in the meeting member's search to understand the actions of another. Though her perceptions differ drastically from mine, her insights broaden my perspective. And I try to respond to the wonder in the worried parent's seeking for a way to support her acting out thirteen-year-old though I know from my experience the adolescent is following very typical patterns. And, when I succeed in responding openly to another's wonder, life gains more meaning and richness for us both. And one marvels that it is so.

Answering that of God in Our Children

And the surprise is that the wondering can be found in the youngest of our children!

Our daughter described how our oldest grandson at birth stared at this world. He was so engrossed he didn't move, he didn't breathe. He just stared at this world of bright lights, colors, and smiling faces around him. He became bluer. The doctor had to give him a sound pat on his bottom to get him to attend to the practicalities of life, namely breathing. He seemed too involved in the wonder, the marvel, of this new world around him. This child still becomes engrossed visually.

Two-day-old babies, scientists find using all their fancy gadgets, are attempting to make sense out of their worlds. The length of time they fixate varies depending if they are shown two different colors in contrast to two hues of the same color. At this early age infants are seeking to organize, to make sense out of, their world. At this elementary level of looking for similarities in colors, they are starting their search for understanding and meaning.

Infants, seeking their role, learn it quickly if the people in their environment are cooperative. They cry in discomfort whether hungry, uncomfortable, tired or bored. And as their cry is answered they learn their newborn's role is to cry when in distress. A few weeks later they learn another role. A smile will bring forth a smile and maybe even an interchange of cooing, if there is another to join in the game.

Our search reveals the Inner Light in every child. For me that means revealing the wondering in each child in its different forms: the marveling, the searching to understand, and the seeking one's path. It is so easy to miss infants' wondering because the content about which they wonder is so elementary, simple, basic. Children, too, use these wonderings to grow into goodness. We are less inclined to see them as growing into goodness when they play with their food or come home sad from the ball game. But they are searching to understand and seeking to find the way as much as we adults. Only the content of their search differs. Their explorations are of their immediate physical world; our search is of the abstract spiritual one. But we all are looking to find meaning in our lives, to find truth by which to live. We all want to know what we can and, eventually, should be doing.

Seeing my child as a wonderer with the potential of growing into goodness expands my understanding of that child and defines my role as parent or caregiver. I can be a loving guide rather than a strict authority figure or just a loving companion. The following stories, drawn from life, illustrate the wondering that our children do and the role it opens for us who live and work with them.

I watched my eight-month-old grandson, Lennen, finishing a banana. As he munches the last hunk, he picks up the peel, waves it back and forth, shakes it vigorously, and then brings it down hard against the metal bowl lying on the floor and, now that his mouth is relatively empty, puts the peel in his mouth and tries to bite. The peel comes out quite quickly and is dropped as his eyes wander to the wooden spoon nearby. He grabs the spoon, raises it high and brings it down hard against the metal bowl. It makes a resounding clang. That stroke is repeated; my grandson smiles and giggles. Then he tries waving the spoon; the movement is awkward compared to waving the banana peel. He drops the spoon and waves the banana peel, getting it to flap in a way the spoon did not do. The banana peel is dropped as the child reaches over to pick up the spoon. The reach is long; he braces himself with one hand coming to rest on top of the banana peel which starts to slide. He looks at the banana peel and tried the sliding motion again and again and again.

At this point his dad says "The banana peel is slippery, isn't it, Son? It slides when you push it." The boy then picks up the spoon and tried to slide it across the floor. His dad laughs, "The spoon doesn't slide, does it?"

Ten-month-old Sara wiggled over towards Nat. She reached out grabbing his cheek in a tight pincher grasp. Nat cried out. Sara's face wrinkled up as if she might cry too as she continued to hold on. Mother ran, picking up Nat as she sat down next to Sara saying, "Oh Sara, Sara. This is Nat. He doesn't like to be grabbed. Here, stroke his head this way. See how soft it is?" as she gently demonstrated while comforting Nat. Then she took Sara's hand and held it while gently moving her hand back and forth on Nat's head.

The ten-minute walk through the woods to the mailbox took half an hour the summer our second child was one and a half. She had to greet each mushroom and toadstool on the way and it had been a rainy summer. The woods were full of them, black and orange and bright red as well as the usual yellowish white. Some had big flat tops. She was sure she would find a fairy living there. And some had peaked caps like umbrellas, perhaps the home of a leprechaun. They all delighted her.

The two four-year-olds were busy in the block room building a castle. Susy was saying, "We'll make it big. All this area," as she laid out long blocks marking off the dimensions of the castle to be. "You," she said to her friend Mary, "can start building up the walls. I'll start the bridge here."

"But I want to make a tower," countered Mary.

"We're not ready to make a tower," said Susy. "You have to make the walls first."

"Then why don't you work on the walls, too?" Mary responded. "They're hard; they keep falling down."

"But we want to get finished, don't we?" argued Susy, her voice raising a decibel in pitch. "If we both work on walls, we won't get done. Yesterday we weren't half finished when it was time to clean up." Susy was already laying up blocks for her bridge.

"Oh, I don't want to build a castle," said Mary disgustedly. "I don't want to build just walls. I want to build a tower and decorate it with colored blocks on top." And Mary turned to another part of the block room.

"You spoil everything." Susy's voice was loud and angry. "You said you would. We said we'd build a big castle."

"What's going on, girls?" asked their teacher. "You both sound pretty upset."

"Mary said yesterday she would build a big castle with me but now she won't."

"Susy wants me to build just walls. I want to build a tower."

Both girls were near tears.

"That's pretty disturbing to both of you, isn't it?" the teacher started cautiously. Both girls nodded their heads, tears welling up in their eyes. "Well, now, let's see . . . I guess one thing to get clear is do you want to build together?"

"Yes," said each girl simultaneously, "But . . ."

"No, I just need to know what your goals are. Do you both want to build a castle?"

Again the answer was a simultaneous "Yes, but . . ."

"Then what are your choices?"

"I can build the bridge while Mary builds the walls."

"But I don't want to build the walls . . ."

"Remember," reminded their teacher, "we're just thinking of choices."

"I can build a tower at one corner while Susy builds a bridge and then we can fill in the walls."

"Another choice."

"I could build the bridge and Susy can build the walls."

"But I don't want to build the walls," Susy interjected, the tears welling up in her eyes.

"Remember, we're just thinking of choices."

"We could both build the walls and then I could build my tower and Susy could build the bridge."

"What good thinking! You have five choices as to how you could build your castle working together. Which one will you follow?"

"Neither of us wants to build the walls," summarized Mary. "So we should do them together. Let's build the tower and bridge first and then the walls, if there is time." Turning to Susy she added, "You've outlined the castle so we know where the bridge and tower need to go."

"O.K." Susy agreed reluctantly.

"Darn those black kids," yelled eight-year-old Tom slamming the door. "They spoil everything."

"What happened?" called his mother. "I'm in the bedroom sorting laundry. You sound really angry."

"We were playing baseball. The usual guys. Then Al and Bob came and insisted on playing. When they started, Joe, Don, and Josh left. They're our best players."

"Why did they leave?"

"They don't like Al and Bob. That's no reason to ruin the game."

"You feel not liking Al and Bob is no reason to stop playing?" Tom nodded.

"Why don't Joe, Don, and Josh like Al and Bob?"

"Al took over the pitching saying he was better than Joe though he's not. And Bob called that he was going to be first baseman, the position Don had been playing. The game was ruined."

"Hey, wait a minute. I'm confused. Who spoiled the game? Do I understand the story correctly? You were all playing happily before Al and Bob came." Tom nodded his head. "When Al and Bob came they took Joe's and Don's places." Again Tom nodded his head. "How did you others feel about that move?" asked his mother. "You say that both Joe and Don are better players in their spots than Al and Bob."

"But you can't argue with Al and Bob. They just keep talking louder and saying we won't be able to play. It's Al's backyard, you know."

"I'm still confused. Who disrupted the game?"

"Joe, Don, and Josh. They left. If those blacks hadn't left we'd still be winning."

"Wait a minute. What if Al and Bob hadn't come, what might have happened?"

"We were ahead . . . looked like we'd win."

"Were there positions open that Al and Bob could have taken?"

"Sure. We needed outfielders but no one likes to play out there."

"What if you others had objected to Al and Bob's moving in?"

"They'd have not let us play. It's Al's field."

"Do you think Al's parents would have allowed that?"

"Ahmm . . . not if they knew."

"Can you really say that Joe, Don, and Josh were the sole cause of the ruined game?"

Tommy looked surprised, then perplexed and confused.

"We discussed the Lord's Prayer today," Pat volunteered in the car on the way home from meeting. "You know we sang it in choir last year. I love the power of that music as it builds. I never really thought about the words. But reading it and thinking about the words . . . I don't know. Why should God give us bread and not people in Somalia? How can God work to change how things happen so we aren't tempted? We had a really hot discussion. Rhoda and Max seemed shocked that we would even question the prayer. Dale thought we were crazy to discuss it. The idea made no sense to him. The rest of us were just confused."

"Stopping to think about the words raises lots of issues, doesn't it?" commented Dad. "I've wondered the same myself."

"You have?" the surprise was apparent in Pat's voice.

"Yes. I find the issue of expecting bread to be given us harder than the idea of not being led into temptation."

"Why?"

"Well, we have been given the ability to think through issues.

Maybe that is God's way of not leading us into temptation. But, as you say, why should we have bread and not people in Somalia?"

"But maybe they should have bread, too, and if we as a world shared better, all would have bread," countered Pat.

"You're suggesting we have a bigger role than just asking for bread," responded Dad, his head nodding.

"Mom," said twelve-year-old Pam as she came into the kitchen from school and opened the refrigerator to find a snack. "What would you say if I told you I was on crack?" Her mother turned from peeling the potatoes and grasped the counter behind her. Looking her child square in the eye, she said, her voice barely audible, "Are you?"

Seeing her mother's reaction, Pam laughed. "Goodness, Mom, of course not. But what would you say?" pushed her daughter.

"Well," her mother tried to gather her thoughts. "I guess I'd feel first. I'd be sad and shocked. I'd be very very sad because crack has such serious consequences. It is so difficult to break the habit and it is very habit forming. And you not only hurt yourself. People on crack do things that hurt others. But why the question?"

"But what would you say and what would you do?" pushed Pam.

"Well, I don't really know. I hadn't thought that one out. I guess I hoped I wouldn't have to face it. I guess I feel you have the judgment not to get involved. I guess I hope if the temptation were getting too strong you'd come and talk with Daddy and me before you tried it." Then Pam's mother smiled broadly at her daughter, "Maybe that is what you are doing now." And Pam nodded.

She poured herself a cup of tea as Pam settled for some milk and cookies and they started talking about: Why people use drugs—it makes them feel good. The effects of drugs on the person—look at what happened to Prince William Sound because one captain of a tanker was drunk. But doctors prescribe drugs—the healthy and unhealthy use of drugs. What one can say when a friend asks you to try drugs—We can go to my house and play Nintendo; my Mom always has snacks on hand. What to do if you are out of an evening and drugs are being pushed—Call, I'll always come and get you. Always have a quarter for a phone call. What did you do when you were my age to feel good?—I had my crafts and music and was busy in activities. What did other kids do?—Kids got drunk even then and the effects could be just as serious. Your grandparents, my parents, warned me about alcohol. I knew they would be sure I was headed for hell, if I got drunk. I also knew I didn't want to risk an accident. My folks let me use their car from an early age, I didn't want to jeopardize that privilege. But somehow it was never a real temptation. Maybe it wasn't so available.

They discussed the latest soap opera where the heroine had started using cocaine and what had happened. Pam confided about a ninth grader on the tennis team who was reported to be using steroids. An hour later Mom returned to peeling potatoes.

Driving his fourteen-year-old son, Ray, and Ray's buddy, Sam, to the Junior Gathering site, Dan was enjoying listening to music when the boys' conversation began to intrude. "The walls are very thin. It would be easy to make just a little hole. Then we could really see." It was Ray speaking. "But how would the girls feel?" Sam asked. "My sisters never want me around when they are dressing."

"Oh girls just say they don't want anyone around. We won't be hurting them. They won't even know," replied Ray. And then he said something else too softly for Dan to hear.

"Boys will be boys," thought Dan, remembering his own escapades as a boy. "And girls are certainly an interesting subject." He went back to listening to the music. But his thoughts kept returning to the boys' conversation. "Yes," he thought, "boys will be boys but do they need to know at this stage how girls feel? When should boys begin to recognize the rights of women?" He thought of the current rape trial when the man agreed the woman had said, "No," but he had interpreted that as just a woman's way of saying, "Yes."

As they arrived at camp, Dan was feeling most uneasy. Should he interfere? He'd overheard the conversation; was that prying? What should he say? Would bringing up the topic make it bigger than it was?

The boys fell out of the car in their haste to join the others, getting tents up and sleeping bags out to mark the spots on which they might sleep.

Dan took the counselor aside and shared the overheard conversation plus all his doubts in doing so. The counselor nodded. "Thanks," he said. "Issues of relationships always come up. It is good to have such information. It can be woven in meaningful ways into our discussions."

Ken, his sister, and their parents were enjoying his favorite dinner. Ken had just arrived home for spring vacation of his junior year in college. He was describing the papers he hoped to finish over vacation and the books he had to read.

"Sounds like a busy vacation, Son—not much of a vacation."

"Yeah, but tonight I am going to take off. Don and Judy are both home. We're going to get together and compare notes. I want to tell them about this woman, Katie, who visited college last week who'd been in the Peace Corps. Oh, I forgot , I haven't told you either. She lived in the Amazon jungle and had to walk into her site. She had to carry her water from a nearby stream and do her laundry in the river. She had to bring all her food in. She found out that she could really rough it."

"Found out she could live off the land, as you say, back to nature. Sounds as if you are very fascinated with the idea. Are you thinking about doing it?

"Yeah," answered Ken with a tentative smile, "But it is more than just being able to rough it. She's helping them. The people in the jungles are less nomadic now that they have schools. They live in clusters; sanitation has become a major problem. She taught them about sanitation and why it was important and helped them build latrines. While doing that she learned that they were selling their handicrafts very cheaply to middle men who came through and then sold them in the city making exorbitant profits. She taught them how to pack their work and take it to the city to sell directly to the merchants. She even had to go with them the first time; some of them had never been to the city. I'd like to do something like that before settling down to a job and family. It seems like a wonderful way to get to know another culture, a developing nation. I think I could contribute something too. I've had Spanish. I could use it. It would be great."

"Does that mean you wouldn't apply to graduate school?" asked Ken's Dad, cautiously.

"Oh, I would go ahead and apply. Katie said it would be easier to do that now and ask for a deferment than to try to apply from wherever I go. Katie had a hard time getting all her papers together to apply from where she was stationed."

"When would you go in?" questioned his Mother.

"Right after graduation next year."

"Had you been thinking of such a step before Katie came to campus? You'd never mentioned it." His Dad's voice was musing in its tone.

"Not really. I didn't know much about the Peace Corps. But it always made sense to me how the Mormons go out in the missionary field for two years before settling down. We Quakers don't proselytize, but we do believe in reaching out to help others. This would be a way of doing so."

"Will this change your plans to become an environmentalist?"

"Going into the Peace Corps will slow them up, but think what I will learn living simply, getting to know the problems of developing nations. Just this week in ecology several of us were irate with the jungle people for burning the trees to plant beans. Katie was there. She reminded us that the pioneers here in the good old U.S.A. did the same things. Made me stop and think. Saving the environment is complex. Seeing the problems from another people's point-of-view will, in the long run, be useful."

"Let's see," laughed Mother. "Where is the Amazon Jungle? Can relatives visit and how soon. I've never thought much about going to South American but I feel a trip is in the offing."

The boys were about two, one three months younger than the other that fall, when we managed to get together. The families live some three hundred miles apart. The boys had anticipated their time together. "Ben coming!" "Go see Lennen!" Such excitement. The mothers, my daughters, and I were no less excited about having time to share.

The boys hugged each other, both nearly knocking the other down in their excitement and standing on their not yet too stable legs. They wandered over to the sand pile. Watching, I, now the grandmother, had a sense of joys being re-experienced and of life going on and of wonder that my daughters had not only produced such healthy little fellows able to participate so fully in life, but that they were able to nurture their children's love of life. The wonder and awe each of us was radiating I recognize now as an outward expression of the Inner Light.

We, my girls and I, were quickly sharing what the boys were each doing, noting their common interests and distinct personalities. We talked about how their different temperaments affected how they were cared for and imagined what the long-term consequences might be. Within an hour our talk was interrupted. The little guys were fighting. Each wanted the red dump truck. Each had a hand on it pulling from the other and crying. Their mothers talked about sharing and gave the truck to whichever boy it seemed to be most appropriate to give it to. By the second day the boys were saying, "Ben not share," while Ben was saying, "Lennen not share." They were both pulling on the same truck.

"What should we do?" my girls asked me. And all I could do was remember similar situations when they were little. "Sharing is hard to understand when you are only two," was my only comment. "I always found it hard at this age."

The next morning the mothers, rested and refreshed, picked up on the situation, "You know I've been thinking about this 'sharing.' To the boys sharing means giving up. That's what happens to them. They have to give up the truck."

Her sister laughed, "You're right. I was thinking the same thing. What can sharing possibly mean? Their understanding of ownership is to have the item in their hands. When we forgot Lennen's favorite book at the child care home last week, he cried. We finally realized he thought the book now belonged to

Thany, the child caregiver's son. After all the book was at Thany's house!"

The other sister nodded. "Ownership is having the truck in your hand. They need to learn steps to sharing as well as how to play together and have fun with just one truck."

"One could load and the other drive as well as taking turns."

"Is this when you started getting us to take turns by using the timer?" one of my daughters asked me.

"I don't remember how old you were but it might be. Having them experience taking turns certainly would mean more to them than just hearing the words."

And we started talking about the steps children need to go through to understand concepts such as sharing and ownership. My children had joined me in seeking how to guide children.

Answering so that Children May Continue Wondering

Children from infancy onward grow into goodness by wondering. They marvel at the beauty of their world and at thoughtful acts. They search to understand how the world works. They seek their way in their world. In each of the previous stories the adults had a choice as to how to respond. The adults, while loving the child, could have been a strict authority figure, only a companion, but rather chose to be a guide.

As a companion to the child in each of the above situations, the adult's actions would have been supportive of the children's explorations but not expansive of them. Sara's mother might have said, "You do find Nat interesting, don't you? He is a wonderful baby." Or Tom's mother might have commiserated, "You really feel bad you lost the game." And Ken's parents would have done what they did without all the questions, they would have supported his plan to go into the Peace Corps but not explored the possible consequences.

As an authority figure the adults could have said:

"Banana peels aren't for eating. Don't slide peels on the floor!"

"Hurry!" ignoring the mushrooms.

And to the four-year-olds, "Build nicely, girls."

"Just say, 'No,' to drugs."

"If you use drugs, you can't live here."

"The Peace Corps is not a career. You're just postponing getting on with your life."

"The Peace Corps is a great idea. You will provide a wonderful service to humankind."

Authorities impose order/discipline/opinions. Too often in our society the order imposed is negative. "Don't hit." "Don't fight." "Don't whine." "Don't slam the door." "Don't leave your books on the dining room table." After reading some books on child rearing with their lists of "Don'ts," I have wondered what *is* the child *supposed* to do.

Viewing children as wonderers gives a different perspective, a different challenge. Children, from this perspective, are scientists trying to figure out what works. They are trying to solve a problem, "If I do this, what will happen?" My grandsons wrestling on the floor are having fun but I know someone will get hurt. That is the consequence. How can I help them anticipate this? How can I help them learn to monitor their wrestling so it is not too rough, or so they can accept the consequence of being hurt or refrain from the activity?

Seeing children as searching redirects our efforts from either ignoring a situation or imposing order to one of searching for ways of guiding them. This perspective leads parents to ask such questions as:

What is my child trying to accomplish?

What does my child understand?

What does s/he need to know?

How much can s/he understand at this time?

What is my child able to do?

What further relevant skills does s/he need?

What is s/he capable of doing at this stage of development?

What do I want my child to learn?

By understanding how ten-month-olds grab any object, animate or inanimate, Sara's mother knew that her daughter was not being aggressive when she reached out for Tommy. This is the way a ten-month-old picks up everything. By asking herself what Sara needed to know, she realized her role. She taught Sara that Tommy was different from a doll and showed her how to touch this other person.

Mary's and Susy's teacher realized the girls were not yet able to solve their conflict. Undoubtedly, he'd helped them go through the process before. But once again he led them to acknowledge their feelings. He helped them identify their goals and brainstorm their options. At that stage of the process Mary was able to take over and suggest a solution.

Tommy's mother had a difficult role. Her understanding of the process of why the team lost the baseball game differed significantly from that of her eight-year-old son. She realized that he, using the thinking style of his age, grouped the boys and their behavior into categories of either all good or all bad. Joe, Ken, and Josh had left so they were at fault. Tom's mother through her questioning encouraged him to think through the event. Thus Tom came to realize other reasons for the boys' leaving the game and other ways the team could have handled the situation. Without telling him, his mother made it possible for Tom to see another possible role for himself, as he sought to understand what was going on around him and his place in it.

For Ken's parents, the same process of guiding children was apparent. Their work was easier than that of Tom's mother. Ken, basically an adult, was able to search out the information he needed to consider the consequences of his action. The parents' role became one of checking, supporting.

With my daughters, now parents themselves, our paths of searching had joined.

All these parents functioned as guides to their children as their children searched to learn about their world and how it works, as they sought to find their place in that world and they marveled at the beauty around them and at the truth as they found it. And the parents became searchers themselves as they sought for ways of guiding their children into goodness.

A belief that children can grow into goodness through a search for truth creates a very different challenge for parents, teachers and meetings than believing children are inherently good or bad. Harold Loukes wrote, "We can thus envisage the process of religious education as not primarily instruction or training, but rather as the creation of the right conditions for growth."[5]

A challenge to create the right conditions for growth leaves much to the imagination and is somewhat daunting in its magnitude. Maybe that is why the topic is so neglected, as Michael Rutter, in his 1983 Swarthmore Lecture, noted that it had been. But, if we are to live and work with children, these conditions must be identified.

I offer here ten commonalties, drawn from the preceding vignettes, that begin the process of defining the "right conditions." Each supports the growth or the attributes Rutter claims our children require:

> The intellectual skills required to work out ways of dealing with social problems (of translating values into practice),

empathy and a concern for others, and the spiritual qualities needed for sorting out values when they are under stress.[6]

Creating an Environment that Nurtures Wonder

1. *Believing there is order in the universe.*   Truth exists. Parents, as they conduct their own search, model for their children Quakers' basic belief in the existence of A Way, that there is Truth for which we seek and which, at least part of, can be found. At first parents illustrate this truth by helping their children understand the physical properties of the world, as the infants were exploring. The underlying message of the teacher of the fours was that there is a way people can work together and here are some of the necessary skills. Pam's mother was saying the same; drugs have very observable effects on one's body; there are healthy and unhealthy ways of using them. And so we can go through each of the vignettes identifying how the parents' beliefs in an underlying order influenced their interaction with their children.

2. *Working from a value system.*   Michael Rutter speaks of parents needing basic values in which they have confidence.[7] In the vignettes, the parents and caregivers used a value system while guiding their children. It dealt with outcome: what were the anticipated effects of the proposed action on the child, others, or the environment? Would they encourage growth in the child? My grandson's father valued the experimenting his son was doing even though the linoleum got sticky. (Notice he did set limits to the experimenting; the banana peel was not on the rug.) Susy's and Mary's teacher was interested that they be able to build together. Pam's mother was concerned that her daughter understand how drugs could affect her and her family.

And Ken's parents explored the outcome of a Peace Corps experience on the people in the jungle as well as on Ken and on his future plans. In all cases the consideration was for the continuing welfare of all those involved, a process which requires empathy, a quality Rutter noted that children need.

I call this value system "caring," which means being concerned about the welfare of another, about the effects of behavior on others, concern about the outcome, wanting the outcome to be beneficial for whoever and whatever is involved.

3.   *Recognizing the Thou* in our children from infancy on. Viewing my child as one who is searching for answers and seeking her way leads me to see the "Thou" in my child, to accept my child as he or she is.

Christ valued children. He told us, "Such is the kingdom of heaven" (Mk. 20:14). Through the years writers have interpreted "such" to mean children's innocence, their naiveté, their dependency, their acceptance. I believe it is their questioning: their wondering how and why and where do I fit in; their seeking to know that this thing slides and this does not; their searching to figure out how to build a castle with a best friend; their attempting to identify all the consequences of using drugs; their broadening their horizons of what is possible. Harold Loukes identifies this questioning as what makes us human; this questioning is the ability to search. It drove Christ at the age of twelve to be at the Temple among the scribes and elders asking them questions and pondering their answers. Viewing people as seekers is an integral component of Quakerism. Our children are fellow participants in that search.

The parent in each of the vignettes recognized the "Thou" in their child. They affirmed the seeking that their children were going through. How easy it is to lose. Only with the work of Jean

Piaget has the psychological world recognized what profound seekers even newborns are.

In the ongoing living with children it is so easy to lose this perspective. Children's behavior is much easier to evaluate from our adult interpretation than to pause and try to see the situation through the eyes of the child. Shortly after our third grandchild was born I was visiting my daughter. Ben, her three-year-old, dashed in from outside. Spying his baby brother lying on the floor, he aimed toward him. Wendilee got there first. "You're glad to see your brother, aren't you Ben? See he just woke up. Would you like to hold him?" Ben nodded. "Sit here. Are you comfortable?" She adjusted his arm to rest on the side of the couch and carefully placed the baby in his lap. "See how he is looking at you, Ben?" Ben nodded as his eyes sparkled with pleasure and pride. "He likes being held by you." Very quickly Ben had had enough of sitting still and was off once again.

"You moved fast," I observed.

"I have to, though it took me a while to learn," Wendilee responded. "He is so attracted to Luke. Any time he sees Luke, he rushes over to give him a big bear hug just like his Dad gives him. I'm afraid he'll hurt Luke and of course Luke cries. At first I reprimanded Ben and tried to keep Luke away from him and out of sight, feeling this was the way to keep sibling rivalry to a minimum. But Ben looked so disappointed, I wondered if he didn't really want to interact with Luke. So then we did this, letting him hold Luke. Ben is so energetic and vivacious I always stay near by. He is gentle and he looks so proud. Now he is starting to bring Luke toys. We talk about what makes a good toy for a baby and what doesn't."

"I wonder," picking up the theme of childrearing that we discuss so often, "how many parents interpret an older child's enthusiastic physical greeting of a new baby as jealousy when actually it is just that, an enthusiastic physical greeting?"

"It is so easy to do. All the books constantly talk about sibling rivalry and jealousy. But when Ben learned how to hold Luke that first time, he was so pleased. He just beamed. Then I knew his actions were not springing from jealousy. He didn't know how to relate to Luke."

Accepting that the older child's too-rough handling of an infant is not jealousy but inexperience does not mean that no action should be taken; the baby needed to be protected, as Wendilee did, while she helped the older child learn how to relate to the very vulnerable, younger child.

Responding to children as seekers, recognizing the Thou in each of them, leads parents to view a situation from their children's points-of-view. It guides parents to consider what the child needs to know and needs to be able to do.

4. *Considering the developmental level of the child,* and, therefore the level of the child's searching. Ten-month-olds need to explore their physical and social world to learn what does what. Wooden spoons, for example, make wonderful noise when banged against metal pots but do not slide well along the floor while banana skins are just the opposite, sliding but not banging. The infant and young child's exploration is concrete, dealing with how objects and people function.

They are seeking to know: What happens if I cry? What happens if I persist? Does the same thing happen the second time? A friend reminded me of her youngest who tasted a piece of uncooked rhubarb and made the wrinkled up face one makes when biting something so sour. He then took another piece, bit and made the same face. On doing the third she started to wonder what was the matter with her child that he didn't learn from the first two pieces that this is the way rhubarb tastes. A young child has to try again and again before knowing that all pieces of things that look alike also usually taste the same. The infant and young child marvel, search, and seek in the realm of the here and now.

As they grow toward toddlerhood they add words to their explorations, putting names to everything and every action. Words add a whole new realm to their wonderings. They add words to their physical expressions of marvel about their world. At this stage the word "crash" can be added when the trucks are jammed together. And "Me do," as the child seeks to find what he or she is capable of. Eighteen-month-old Russell would stand on the sea wall, pointing upward at the seagulls gliding with the breeze, "Burd, burd," we'd hear him call.

Using words expands children's repertoire of ways of dealing with situations. The four-year-olds learned how to deal with their differences verbally. They were learning to understand that others had likes and dislikes as they did themselves.

Elementary school-aged children are still exploring. Now they can do it competently with words. Like eight-year-old Tommy and the baseball game, they are aware of situations and search to understand, but their ability to understand complex relationships is limited. Situations tend to be categorized as good or bad, right or wrong. Tommy blamed the lost baseball game on the black boys who left. He could not analyze the process with its grays and innuendoes that led up to their leaving. For this he needed an adult.

By twelve, Pam is able to explore issues abstractly. What are the effects of drugs? She could search out the various effects of drugs both positive and negative. Able to see the innuendos of good and bad in a way Tommy could not, Pam could start the process of thinking about what role drugs would take in her life. To do so she needed factual accurate information.

The twenty-year-old can explore abstractly the ramifications on his life of living in a different culture and working among people there. He can look at his values and see if his plans are in harmony with them.

They are all seekers, each at her or his own level. Recognizing the level of their search is important as we guide our children.

5.   *Loving them unconditionally* becomes possible when we view our children as seekers. Their actions, so often, are what get in the way of our love. But accepting their actions as their efforts to understand, their attempts to learn, frees me to go on loving as I deal with the situation.

6.   *Trusting our children* is built on recognizing in them their thrust to use their understanding to become competent and to work for the common good. Ben beamed when he was to hold his baby brother. He wanted to know him.

But our trust in our children cannot be "blind." Parents need to recognize the limits of the child's understanding and control. Some newborns being fed, can stop, tightly clamp their mouths shut and appear to be in a deep sleep. Their parents assume from this behavior that the babies are full and ready for a nap. Some babies are and sleep soundly; some babies, upon being moved to their cribs, will give a big burp and be ready for more milk. Parents have to learn what their baby is signaling and how completely to rely on the baby's "decision" as to how full he or she is.

Another early step in learning to trust is when parents recognize that infants will act to prevent themselves from being hurt. The six- to seven-month-old infant, knowing how something "hot" feels, will approach an object so labeled tentatively. Often we do not see this protective behavior in our children because we do not prepare them. We have to give them the information they need on which to base their behavior. I am not sure how I learned that a five- to six-month-old, not yet able to crawl, could learn that things could be "hot." But I do remember, giving each child on reaching that approximate age, uncomfortably warm peas, saying "hot, hot," and demonstrating how to pass one's hand gingerly over the warm food to test the degree of comfort. Each child would mimic my approach. Each child, when he or she started crawling, had an important piece of information for protection when exploring. Food/things could hurt, not that I ever left them near a hot stove. But they did explore a little more cautiously. In similar fashion infants can learn that stairs go up and down and that objects can be sharp. This information that guided their explorations gave me knowledge about how I could trust their ability to protect themselves.

Parents must thoughtfully use the trust they have in their children to guide their behavior. Our two grandsons, within three months of age, are very different. Ben is enthused about life and rushes excitedly into everything. Lennen tends to size up a situation before entering in. The concepts of "hot" or "sharp" or "up and down" moderated Lennen's behavior at a younger age than they did Ben's.

Elementary-school-aged children, organizing their world, as they do, into specific categories that do not blend or overlap, miss the innuendoes and gray areas of a situation. Thus when discussing the baseball game with eight-year-old Tom, his mother trusted that with her guidance Tom would see the situation as more complex, something he was not able to do on his own.

Trusting that the child will make good decisions is scary when the decision involves drugs, becoming sexually active, and all those other issues our young people today have to face. The fear was there in Pam's mother when her child first raised the question and in Ken's parents as they wondered how his new plans would affect his vocation.

My trust in each of my children, I find, is built partially from experiences with the child, knowing how the child thinks and the processes he or she uses to make decisions. Guiding children from babyhood on through age-appropriate experiences of making decisions has deepened my trust.

7. *Providing them with the accurate information and relevant skills* they need for whatever issue and/or situation with which they are dealing. Pam wanted information about drugs. She needed accurate, precise data on which to make her decisions. The four-year-olds' teacher knew these children could learn conflict resolution skills but to do so they had to practice them again and again.

Part of the challenge for parents is recognizing the information and skills needed. It is too easy to take for granted that they have our store of knowledge and skills. Or maybe the problem requires information and/or skills we don't have. I know I never learned to deal well with teasing. This lack as a person has made me vulnerable. It is a vulnerability I have passed on to my children. It would have been a very appropriate time to use outside help.

8. *Listening,* some have called it profound listening, gives children a sense of being heard. It gives parents information about the issues with which their children are dealing. Listening may mean watching behavior as well as taking in the words, as Wendilee did when she moved quickly to help Ben greet Luke.

9. *Giving them time—time to marvel, time to search and to seek.* It takes time to marvel at the beauty of the world or to reflect on

the kindness of another. It is so hard to give our children this time. And we have to give ourselves time as well. I remember how impatient I would get on that half-hour walk to the mailbox, as Wendilee greeted each mushroom and toadstool. It helped if I had my knitting along. Somehow if my hands were busy, I could stop and enjoy all those growing things with my daughter. And children with their schedules of Little League Baseball and violin lessons, sleepovers, and homework have little time to look at the full moon or the buds coming on the trees. Nor do we, their parents, with our schedules of work, social commitments and family life, take time ourselves.

10. *Encouraging the searching and the seeking* by allowing it, modeling it, and teaching it in age-appropriate ways to the young in their care. Children have to learn many of the skills of searching for their way. It is true the early exploratory ones, as those exhibited by the ten-month-old grabbing the other infant, are there if the infant is not restrained. Even these need refinement, how to explore without hurting. But the more complex ones such as the intellectual skills mentioned by Rutter, must be learned, as the teacher of the four-year-olds demonstrated. Pam's mother and Ken's parents modeled communication skills that kept the dialogue open. Ken's parents' role had become one of supporting a process that Ken seems to have mastered well.

The children's behavior was guided, not controlled. By demonstrating "hot," I gave my five-month-old an important piece of information on which to base his future exploring when he could crawl, namely, things can hurt. But explore they did. With Lennen the guidance was only to direct his attention to what was happening. Sara learned that infants were different from objects and how to start to relate to them. The teacher of the four-year-olds did not settle the dispute for the girls but helped them go through a problem-solving process that helped them settle their problem. The mother of eight-year-old Tommy made him look more closely at what had actually occurred to ruin the baseball game. The mother of the twelve-year-old girl did not preach the danger of drugs but explored with her daughter the possible outcomes, drawing on experiences they had shared including soap operas.

These parents, recognizing all three components of wondering—marveling, searching for understanding and seeking to find the path for them—set up right conditions in their children's environments for their children's growing into goodness.

Quaker discipline is more a process of guidance than of imposing one's will. It emphasizes helping the child understand rather than just passively accepting the whys of a situation. It encourages a child to search for understanding and meaning rather than follow rules and regulations blindly.

> ### Creating an Environment that Nurtures Wonder
>
> 1. *Believing there is order in the universe*
> 2. *Working from a value system*
> 3. *Recognizing the Thou in our children*
> 4. *Considering the developmental level of the child*
> 5. *Loving them unconditionally*
> 6. *Trusting our children*
> 7. *Providing them with accurate information and relevant skills*
> 8. *Listening*
> 9. *Giving them time—time to marvel, time to search, and time to seek.*
> 10. *Encouraging the searching and the seeking*

And the Wondering Comes Full Circle

Parents, creating environments that nurture, find themselves wondering. The parents in the vignettes marveled at their children. How could eight-month-old Lennen be so systematic in his testing the banana skin and the wooden spoon? Isn't it amazing that ten-month-old Sara would choose Nat to immediately wiggle over to? And how could Tom blame Joe, Don, and Josh and not see Al's and Bob's role in ruining the baseball game? Ken's parents could not help but marvel that their son could manage the Amazon, that their son saw this opportunity for service.

The parents searched to understand their children. Is this how a ten-month-old reaches for something? What do these four-year-olds need so that they can build happily together? What is Tommy's understanding of the reasons why the game was lost? Is my child on drugs? What is Pam trying to understand? And is our son Ken's understanding of the consequences of his joining the Peace Corps thorough enough?

Meaning and purpose to life grow out of this search to understand our children. We experience that their learning how the physical world works parallels their later understanding of more abstract situations such as peer relationships. We come to recognize the importance of our insights being mixed with those of our children as new visions emerge.

And the parents sought to determine what their role should be. Is Sara old enough to understand if I show her how to touch Tom? How can I give Wendilee time to enjoy the mushrooms and not spoil it by my impatience? How can I help Ben relate to his baby brother? How much do I reveal my own thought about the Lord's prayer? Do I have a role in Ray's weekend, especially as the conversation, discussing how they could peek at the girls, was overheard? How can we ask Ken about his decision without undermining him as a person?

I come back to another verse in the song quoted earlier:

> I wonder as I wander with a child by my side;
> His seeking, her searching, how can I be their guide?
> So much I don't know; Their questions spur mine
> To wonder as I wander with a child by my side.

Seeking to find the right conditions for our children in the time and space in which we live gives me a sense of continuity to that which has gone before and that which is now.

As a small child I spent a month with my mother's mother in Omaha, six-hundred miles from our home. All her children were grown. We must have brought into her house noise and dirt and junk. But I do not remember being reprimanded. What I do remember is her attempt to always find me a girl friend as the cousins were all boys. She was seeking those right conditions.

Memories of my mother's search are numerous. I was a challenge to her. In contrast to her interests I loved trying to make things out of nothing. Not only did that mean a continuous mess but it meant keeping me supplied with the "nothings," tallow for candles, materials for puppets, yarn for knitting. Every Saturday morning Mother and I had a routine. We changed the sheets so the beds would be clean for people after they had had their Saturday night baths. We baked pies and nut bread, cake and cookies. As we worked we talked of school and what people did, of what was kind and what was not, of what should be and what should not. There was nothing we did not discuss during our Saturday morning routine. Our looking together at issues, our searching to understand, and our seeking for solutions continued into my adult life and motherhood. It lasted until her too early death. And one of the great losses of her early dying has been that I could not ask her about what she thought and felt as I passed down the path of parenting on which she had walked before.

And now I see my daughters. They do not nurture their children as I did. They nurture them as I would were I to start over. I listen to their dialogue and wish the insights had been mine when they were the age of their sons. But I am also part of the dialogue.

The phone rings. "Mom," Annemarie's voice is tight, "Lennen bit a child at the daycare home yesterday. She won't keep him if he starts biting."

"Oh, that's serious."

"Yeh," the reply was faint.

"But he hasn't made a pattern of it yet. What happened?"

And she began describing the situation, telling me the events that had led up to the biting. Then we began thinking about what Lennen might have been trying to accomplish and what behavioral alternatives he had. Together we were searching to understand and seeking to find a way. We knew there was a way. My daughter's wondering and mine had joined. Her insights add to mine. I see in my mind's eye a connectedness from grand-mother to mother to me and now to daughters and a connected-ness from infant to child to youth to adulthood, and old age. And the song continues:

> We wonder as we wander, my children and I
> The beauty and the glory that around us doth lie.
> Each seeks for her path as our search intertwines
> As we wonder as we wander, my children and I.

And I feel a certain certitude that this might be the Inner Light visible within us all, young and old alike, this searching to understand and seeking to find our way while daring to marvel that it is so. I feel an inner acceptance that by responding and relating to the Inner Light in the other as best we can we are answering to that of God in every person.

Notes

1. Rutter, Michael, *A Measure of Our Values: Goals and Dilemmas in the Upbringing of Children* (London: Quaker Home Service, 1984), p. 6.

2. Nickalls, John, editor, *The Journal of George Fox* (Philadelphia: Religious Society of Friends, 1985), p. 263.

3. Loukes, Harold, *Friends and Their Children* (London: Friends Home Service, 1969), p. 26.

4. Loukes, Harold, *The Castle and The Field* (London: George Allen, and Unwin, Ltd., 1959), pp. 15–16.

5. Loukes, *The Castle and The Field*, p. 26.

6. Rutter, *A Measure of Our Values*, p. 41.

7. Rutter, *A Measure of Our Values*, p. 41.

ORDER FORM

Yes, please send me a subscription to Pendle Hill pamphlets.

NAME _______________________________________

ADDRESS ____________________________________

CITY _______________ STATE ____ ZIP __________

One year (6 issues) $13.00 ————

Two years (12 issues) 25.00 ————

Three years (18 issues) 36.00 ————

Please send a gift subscription to:

NAME _______________________________________

ADDRESS ____________________________________

CITY _______________ STATE ____ ZIP __________

GIFT CARD FROM _____________________________

ENCLOSED $ ________

For extra copies of this pamphlet or a complete list of publications, please write to:

PENDLE HILL PUBLICATIONS
Wallingford, PA 19086-6099
(610) 566-4514 or 1-800-742-3150